Rambles through the Heart
and Other Regions

Rambles through the Heart
and Other Regions

An Excursion of Poems

RAYMOND H. HAAN

RESOURCE *Publications* • Eugene, Oregon

RAMBLES THROUGH THE HEART AND OTHER REGIONS
An Excursion of Poems

Copyright © 2022 Raymond H. Haan. All rights reserved. Except for brief quotations in critical publications or reviews, no part of this book may be reproduced in any manner without prior written permission from the publisher. Write: Permissions, Wipf and Stock Publishers, 199 W. 8th Ave., Suite 3, Eugene, OR 97401.

Resource Publications
An Imprint of Wipf and Stock Publishers
199 W. 8th Ave., Suite 3
Eugene, OR 97401

www.wipfandstock.com

PAPERBACK ISBN: 978-1-6667-3878-0
HARDCOVER ISBN: 978-1-6667-9988-0
EBOOK ISBN: 978-1-6667-9989-7

MARCH 21, 2022 1:02 PM

Remembering Claretta
(1940–2021),
a gift to me for sixty-two years

Contents

Acknowledgement | ix
Introduction | xi

Rambles through the Heart | 1
The Greatest of These | 2
Friends | 3
Fresh from the Wrapper | 4
Information | 6
Lost | 7
Escaping Bingo | 8
Prejudice | 9
Irresistible Frigidity | 11
Balance | 12
Do You Wonder? | 13
Search for Symmetry | 14
Nocturne | 15

Eight Poems at the End of Claretta's Life

I	Memory	17
II	Plea	18
III	Malediction	19
IV	Her Quiet Room	20
V	Grief	21
VI	Release	22
VII	Silent Walk	23
VIII	No Contest	24

August Joy | 25

Privacy | 26

Crab Trees | 27

Advice | 28

Ach! Ach! Poor Mr. Bach | 29

Three Valentines

I   Heartless on February 14 | 30

II   Cupid's Advice | 31

III   Valentine | 32

Today's Leadership | 33

Air | 34

The Truth and Nothing but the Truth | 35

Tomato | 36

Daydreams | 38

Confession | 39

Lineage of Learning | 40

Prayer for Today | 41

Design | 42

November | 43

Wings | 44

Squabble | 46

Doxology | 47

Lonesome | 48

Riddle Pie | 49

Evening Advice | 50

Self-Portrait | 51

Ecclesiastical Polity | 52

Spizzerinctum | 53

Timepiece | 54

Faith | 55

Resurrection | 56

Acknowledgement

THIS SMALL BOOK CONTAINS only five to six thousand words. They are the moving parts required to convey the freight of half a hundred thoughts and emotions, and they should move together in one direction—wheels under the train of thought. A cardinal requirement for any writer is to put the right word in the right place. As simple as that sounds, it can cause any careful author a good deal of struggle. Since that struggle sometimes blurs the author's vision or induces myopia, another pair of clear and questioning eyes becomes invaluable. For this volume those perceptive eyes belong to Kathleen Herrema, whose insight prevented both words and thoughts from derailment. For her patient and penetrating vision I am most grateful.

Introduction

HEARTS HAVE NO TEMPLATE. They vary as much as snowflakes. Like snowflakes some hearts are cold, but others are warm as babies' hands. Some are grey with melancholy, some bright with good cheer. Some are profound, some simple, some retiring or reclusive, and some full of sweet welcome. The heart holds power, ruling over eyes and lips, thoughts and acts, affections and aversions. Of course, no one sees into another's heart, though lovers claim to hold that joy.

The heart is an elusive organ: neither science nor theology has discovered its location. Yet no one doubts or denies its existence. We describe some people as heartless, by which we mean that their hearts have been so perverted by insensitivity or cruelty as to be invisible. But they, too, have hearts—shadowy organs, small and steely.

I have never met an authority on the mysteries of the human heart, but that is hardly a surprise. Jeremiah said of the heart, " . . . who can know it?" (Jeremiah 17:9b). Though we cannot measure the spectrum of good and evil in the heart—even in our own—each of us understands something of the heart. But rather than attempt to describe or define the human heart, it is better to trace some of its pains, pleasures, and oddities. These pangs and pleasures likely represent what Solomon calls "the issues of life" (Proverbs 4:23). This little volume does not presume to serve as a catalogue of issues drawn up from the heart's well; nor is it a manual for guarding the heart, as Solomon advises. It simply offers a few poems that reflect some of the heart's delight and struggle. Some of these poems are indirect, merely suggesting the presence of the heart. Some are admittedly frivolous, as hearts can be; others are drawn from deep wells. Yet others squeeze into the group, altogether heartless, having slipped in between pulsations.

Rambles through the Heart

Invitation to a Constitutional

The human heart has such terrain
as one will find on rambles:
it's graced with flowers wild and fair
but sometimes fraught with brambles.

An amble through the human heart
with ears and eyes attentive
might well postpone some doctor's call
and preclude his preventive.

The Greatest of These

Like an ever-lengthening string of pearls
moves the long progression of our years,
each year a pearl, each pearl a marvel,
a cherished sphere of shining luster,
glowing richly or demurely in the memory.

This lineage of gems, this wealth of jewels,
is made pleasing in design and lovely in allure
    by one indispensable thing,
        both supple and perfect in length
            and gently tenacious in strength:
                a single, invisible string.

Friends

The clutch of dead December pampas grass sways tall and tan,
like giant bottle brushes in the fitful wind.
Just below the tawny tuft of one thin, quivering stem
swings a clinging chickadee.

Up and down, to and fro
rides the lone and silent bird,
bobbing and circling,
circling and bobbing,
happy in the easy motion,
happy in the slanting sunshine.
For long minutes it rides
to and fro, up and down,
almost, it seems, entranced by joy.

Then, one sudden flash of black and white,
it hurls itself against the sky.

Empty now, the lonesome stem
still bends, still bows
to puffs and fidgets of inconstant wind.

"Come back! Come back!" I seem to hear,
"I'll be your friend."

Fresh from the Wrapper

A Reverie

As you slip the gum from its wrapper,
its welcoming scent coaxes you
to put it quickly into the warm intimacy of your mouth.
Meeting the eager friendship of your teeth,
the gum grows supple and pliant,
and delights you with its fragrance and flavor.

Eventually, though, the flavor fades
and the gum grows less pliant;
it feels worn out, and you decide to put it away.
So, you take it in your fingers,
thinking to put it back into the wrapper.
But you find that the gum, now less moist,
adheres determindly to your fingers.
In fact, it refuses to be pulled or shaken off.
Now you moisten it a bit
and twist it about with your fingers
until at last you manage to roll it into the wrapper.

The gum, though, still has life.
Yes, the juices of its youth are dried,
its first enticing fragrance has much diminished,
and its tired body lacks a trim and tidy contour.
But there it huddles in the wrapper,
recalling the happiness it had and the happiness it gave,
remembering its time of triumph,
its time of sweetness and joy.
It feels sad, now, to be outworn and laid aside,
and it dreams of transformation,
imagining the delight of emerging once more,
fresh from the wrapper to another eager welcome.

Meditatively you finger the wrapper,
wondering, perhaps, how happy you might be
to begin once more:
once more to remove that wrapper
and once again to savor the sweetness of that willing friend.
And, yes, perhaps you wonder, as well,
about the truth of the ancient adage,
Omnia vincit amor.[1]
After all, a weary soldier conquers little—
and a worn-out Cupid can miss his mark.

---

1. "Love conquers all," also rendered, *Amor vincit omnia.*

Information

The heart
is the part
fond lovers take
              poetically.

The heart
will soon smart
if lovers love
              synthetically.

No dart
strikes a heart
stubbornly sealed
              hermetically.

No heart
torn apart
can be repaired
              cosmetically.

No art
heals a heart
just brought to break
              frenetically.

Lost

Circling and crying,
crying and circling,
a lone goose courses
the cloudy grey of evening.

The impassive sky keeps silence.

Crying and circling,
circling and crying,
desperate for an answer
to its raucous call,
it craves companionship
for the flight it still must take.

Cold silence rules the solid sky.

Circling and crying,
crying, crying,
it tears the unresponsive air
with wild, incessant, useless prayer.

Escaping Bingo

Wistful walks the old man
toward the paling sun;
tired thoughts he traces,
treasuring each one.

Pensive strolls the old man
through sun's dying streams;
heartsick, he, and empty,
dreaming withered dreams.

Prejudice

My family members in general
do not relish tomatoes;
most of them do not eat tomatoes.
They possess a prejudice of palate
quite dissimilar to mine.

Coming into the kitchen with a glorious specimen
of the pineapple variety, fresh from the vine,
I am consoled to find two fellow tomato lovers, after all.

I pare away a blemish from this huge yellow, red-capped fellow—
and there they are: an earwig and a tiny slug.
I slowly, ambivalently assist their departure,
knowing, first, that they possessed the tomato before I did
and, second, that they take joy similar to mine
in savoring this succulent summer fruit.

Maybe some would criticize me
for displacing the original settlers,
perhaps labeling me prejudicial, unloving, or even racist.
(No, emphatically, they are *not* illegal immigrants;
they are definitely indigenous,
their ancestors having established residence here
long before my time or the time of my forefathers.
So, at least, I escape the allegation that I am persecuting aliens.)
Still, I deport those original settlers from my tomato.

As I enjoy my juicy blessing,
a question courses through my mind:
since happiness comes from enjoying things with others,
and since no family member
enjoys this flavorful phenomenon with me,
why *did* I deport those enthusiastic guests?

Well.

Perhaps my heart holds bias, after all,
 however hidden and however small.

Irresistible Frigidity

    Hopeless,
        like a foolish child,
            tongue stuck tight
                to some cold, enticing,
                    tongue-seducing
                icy metal,
            I can't get free
        and try to cry,
   Grow warm! Grow warm
and rescue me!

Balance

Today we view the lone and sturdy sapling,
planted a few years past in the landscape of our home.
Watered and tended by your care,
it promises beauty and shade for coming years,
its May-green foliage shining fresh in morning sun.

We notice, though, that winter's winds have not been kind.
Maybe last November's blasts or recent winds, persisting,
have caused our youthful tree to lose some balance,
lean a bit, and look less straight.

A stake, perhaps, might give some help—
a sturdy stake, attached with scraps
of hose and wire, attached with care—
and that should hold it firm and tight,
should keep it straight, unyielding, right.

But are we sure a stake will help our tree?
That stake, however firm and strong,
might cause the roots to fail their work—
and only roots can make a tree,
make it strong and healthy, make it right inside,
and hold it well in place through storms to come.

We want our little tree to grow up straight
but fear to weaken it with help too firm,
and so we ponder in perplexity.
At last we see that Mr. Kilmer had it right:
that, truly, only God can make a tree—
and make it quite precisely what it ought to be.

Do You Wonder?

For most of us these days air conditioning
seems more like a requirement for worship
than a mere comfort;

and some of us find that the sermon goes down better
when we cultivate it with coffee;

and some view thickly-padded pews
as fundamental for perfecting praise.

 Ah! how we relish our comforts.

Do you wonder how long will it be before somebody
asks for butter on his communion bread?

Search for Symmetry

Two legs, two arms,
two calves and thighs,
two feet, two hands,
two ears and eyes,

two palms, two knees,
two heels and hips,
two elbows, wrists,
and praying lips—

but just one heart
sighs deep within,
one lonesome heart
that craves a twin.

Nocturne

I sit alone in the half dark of my room
as the day spins itself away.
The spirit hangs bedraggled, like a tired dog's tail.
Dvorak brings some cheer and solace with his Ninth,
even with the fetching melancholy of the second movement.

I recall singing that sad, caressing melody as a young boy,
dressed, like the rest of my class, in Dutch garb at the Chicago Railroad Fair.
In those days classical music was still a presence in society, even on AM radio.
Every morning my father tuned to the 400 *Hour* with host Norman Ross,
and his theme music from Tchaikovsky's *Swan Lake*
floated thinly from the kitchen as Dad busied himself making our breakfast.
Those days held good things for our family:
excursions to Munster for frozen custard, trips to zoos and museums,
and once to the wonders of Orchestra Hall for *Messiah* at Christmas.
We had no tree at Christmas, but there was always a present for each of us,
and one Christmas my astounding gift was a small rubber army tank
with rubber wheels and a turret that actually turned.
And always there came a Christmas box from Aunt Mimi,
our childless aunt in California—
a box with dates and olives and nuts and clothes—and, maybe, toys.

Yes, Dvorak. I remember teaching this symphony
to the restless adolescents in my care.
I see them now at their desks
in the crowded rows of the small school room.
Some simply listened or endured, but the eyes of others grew far away
as the music touched a deep place inside them.

The beguiling theme returns.
Now comes the exquisite moment of sadness,
that moment when, it seems, the music can no longer move on:
it chokes with emotion and needs to collect itself,
to catch its breath and push away a tear
before resuming its beguiling melancholy.

So it is, sometimes, before we can move on.
We need to catch our breath and collect our strength—
tonight just strength enough to nudge away a lonesome tear,
get up, and ease into the comfort of my cool and soothing sheets.

Eight Poems at the End of Claretta's Life

Spring, 2021

I

Memory

When blossoms dry,
how soon is spent
the savor of
the lilac's scent.

So memory
dissolves and dies,
like rose perfume
or lovers' sighs.

II

Plea

to the Holy Spirit

>Day
>after day
>dark
>burdens weigh,
>
>day
>after day
>fear
>wants to prey,
>
>day
>after day
>fiends
>bleat and bray.
>
>*Shine,*
>*shine today*
>*on*
>*this dark way.*

III

Malediction

He hath sent me to bind up the brokenhearted,
to proclaim liberty to the captives,
and the opening of the prison to them that are bound.

LUKE 4:18

Go, horrid devils that twist
each smiling memory,
every happy picture,
to ugliness and fear.

Go, vile demons that bind my mind,
that steal the freedom of my peace,
that seek to chain my spirit
in your choking and unholy hell.

Go, hideous tormentors,
go with your own searing fears
and let them scorch your fiendish minds.
Go, live in gasping terror
of the hideous burning bondage that awaits
every shrieking moment of your accursed eternity.

IV

Her Quiet Room

How quiet that room—strangely still.
Only an occasional voice—muffled, indistinct—
or a strange, half-distant sound
filters through the odd derangement there.
Shades darken the windows
so that the disorder of the place
makes odd configurations in the gloom.
One last shade admits a fragment of light—
one small shade, not fully drawn,
waiting, it seems, for a gentle tug.

V

Grief

Tonight my mind perversely
    lingers on things dark and sharp—
        as does the creamy half-moon,
lingering supine on the
        jagged, prickly pinnacle
    of a black-shrouded spruce tree.

VI

Release

God, hear my heart's
profoundest plea:
break her bondage,
soon turn the key—
and turning,
set her spirit free.

VII

Silent Walk

Deep stillness tonight—nature holds a long breath:
no chirping of birds, no swish of leaf—heavy silence,
      like that quiet within
        her new-closed coffin.

VIII

No Contest

I had taken a long leap from the starting block
two years before she entered the race,
but eventually she caught up, showing little exhaustion.
After that we ran as a pretty well-matched team,
though our styles showed little resemblance.

I think the spectators, judging from my early lead
and observations of my headlong style,
presumed that I would be the first to reach the finish line.
She, being far more patient than I
and much more like the intelligent tortoise in the fable,
was favored to run long and steadily,
having less concern about the course
and little concern with winning or losing.
After all, we were running on the same team.

Lately it became clear that our knowledge of racing
and our presumptions about it were incomplete and inaccurate.
For, as it turned out, she put on a most uncharacteristic last-minute sprint,
left me well behind, and gracefully won first prize—
or, better, won the prize first.

I am slower now, and sometimes I get muscle cramps,
but I am not a sore loser.
On the contrary, I wish I could have crowned her with a bit of
fragrant laurel as she slipped over the line.
As things were, though, it was impossible
to congratulate her at the moment of victory,
impossible to tell her how thankful I was
for her astonishing, inconceivable speed.
Well, opportunity for that is coming.

August Joy

August now.
Lonesome crickets creak,
and dry, soft-waving grasses gossip in the wind.
Skittish sparrows chirp in eaves and trees,
sometimes a sassy blue jay scolds,
but silence rules the robins' roost.
The cardinal, now stingy with his cheer,
keeps mostly out of sight,
and chickadees perch soundless in the trees.
Even gabby grackles with their angry eyes
have grown invisible.
And so, the world seems quite bereft of birds,
devoid of avian color, song, and motion.

But now a rush of flight comes to the eye:
a lone and lilting thistle-happy finch
bounds and bounces through the heavy air—
a sunny, blissful ball of yellow joy.
A gift he is, for in this cheerless world,
this somber place of dull and waning summer,
we welcome joy of any size or color.

Privacy

Barn owl,
silent in flight,
labors a limp squirrel
into a dark pine to relish
last rites.

Crab Trees

Grey, arthritic boughs,
scabby, misshapen, nurture
spectacular pink.

Advice

Oh, chemists—with your steaming viols,
your beakers, all your gleaming,
complicated apparatus—
with your tables and your calculations,
with your elements, your compounds,
all your fabrications—
go, breathe in the lilac or the rose;
examine well the complex mystery
of fragrance perfect in profound simplicity.

Ach! Ach! Poor Mr. Bach

Although he heard it say tich-toch,
our great and noble Mr. Bach
could hardly read his mantle cloch,
for cataracts his eyes did bloch

When phony surgeon Doctor Taylor
took his blood, Bach just grew paler.
John pricked and cut, and Bach grew frailer.
Yet John escaped the local jailer.

"Oh, rot his sochs!" cried all the Bachs.
"Oh, give his nob some potent knochs
and give his nose some holy sochs!
Begin his shaggy ears to bochs!"

But dear J. S. just said, "Ach! Ach!"
He slowly donned his Sunday froch,
then nipped a nip of Private Stoch
and left for church to play some Bach.

> *Bach suffered from cataracts, and in desperation he permitted two painful and disastrous operations in 1750 at the hands of an itinerant English shyster, John Taylor. Some suspect that Bach's death four months later was the result of John Taylor's questionable methods and incompetent botching.*

Three Valentines

I

Heartless on February 14

(An Explanation for the Valentine I Cannot Give)

> To me today quick Cupid flew.
> No arrow did he fire:
> his sharpened dart could find no heart
> to pierce with love's desire.
> Away he flew—no more to do.

You stole my heart, sweet thief of mine,
and so you stole your valentine.

II

Cupid's Advice

*(to any love-sick but frustrated male
seeking to be a doctor of hearts)*

The female heart is most complex
within its arcane apparatus.
You, doctor, (urgent, yet perplexed
to ascertain its subtle status)
must quench all latent wrath at her,
must shun your shiny stethoscope,
hang up your kinky catheter—
and grip the wispy cord of hope.

III

Valentine

(Confession and Plea)

Like sticky doggie doo,
stinking under queenly heel,
that's exactly how I feel—
obscenely stuck on you.

Perhaps you'll sniff and scoff,
rail or shudder at my thought,
shun it as a thing of naught—
but please don't scrape me off.

Today's Leadership

I make the curve from the expressway
to the one-lane off-ramp
surrounded by low concrete walls.
Watch out!
Mama Duck stands, bewildered,
in the middle of the lane,
her scattered brood straggling on the right side.
I cannot stop, so I veer left,
hoping that she will not move.

Well, she survives, but I will not look back
to view again that concrete trap and hapless ducks.
Why did Mama lead them there?
Surely, her instinct is more potent than her brain,
but neither instinct nor brain steered her from this awful place.
So, Mama, always attentive, always watchful,
led her trusting brood to danger—and likely into death.

That microcosm of calamity,
created by a mother duck astray,
brings me both comfort and distress today:
at least the duck bears no depravity.

Air

The blacksmith's fire requires a bellow's breath,
as does the organ's might and majesty.
The lusty lungs of puff-cheeked tuba players
push music from their cold and silent brass.
The dog delights in swiftly-rushing air—
it points its nose aloft, wind whips its hair.

Without a breeze the whirling windmill halts,
an airplane needs the open, breathing skies,
no skill can coax an airless tire to roll,
and flat balloons are not balloons at all.
So, air brings beauty, air brings joy and life
to countless things and creatures, great and small.

And air it is that causes love to live,
sweet air that clears and dries the tear-blind eye,
brings strength to hand and confidence to heart.
Air is the gentle Spirit's mighty breath,
the exhalation of the Spirit's power.
Without it comes not love—but certain death.

The Truth and Nothing but the Truth[2]

Judge:

"You're living grand,
so you must pay,
pay for your Cadillac
and costly cummerbunds."

Crafty Man of Wealth:

"Someday I'll pay,
I'm sure I'll pay.
But, happily,
you'll understand
and certainly
not reprimand
when now I say
that as things stand
(concerning Cadillac
and summer cummerbunds),
I'm suffering from lack
of insufficient funds."

2. *This poem is meant only as a game for the reader: to see how many readings it takes to know what the man of wealth intends.*

Tomato

After the frost, when summer warmth began,
the tiny wisps began to grow,
and eagerly they burgeoned into sturdy, spreading plants.
At last the fruit appeared—
tiny green globes, pushing out from yellow blossoms.
But the little spheres seemed almost miserly.
Refusing to fill out and become plump, edible fruit,
they clung to their hard, green smallness.
Day followed day. I watered and I hoped:
How long will it be? When will the time come?
Day followed day. No tint, no blush appeared.

At last I began to consider the plants as anomalies,
as freaks or hybrids destined never to ripen.
Then, overnight, mysteriously,
appeared a modest blush of orange—
a tinge, a touch, a hint.
Yet day followed day—and no redness, no ripening.
How long will it be? When will the time come?
Their inner timetables seemed to ignore
the encouraging heat of August,
seemed to disregard my constant watering.

But then, most wonderfully, the time did come—
the day designed by God's tomato clock.
Gently I plucked the first fruit,
round and red in perfect ripeness,
and held it warm in my hand.

Looking at that wonder of ripeness,
I thought again about God's infinitely intricate clock,
set for the perfect ripening of every ripening thing.
And then I recalled that in His hand God holds
His first, last, largest, and most-cherished tomato—
this round and slowly-ripening world.
That ripening, Lord, how long, how long must it be?

Daydreams

Sun-washed yesterdays
wink in wind-silvered wrinkles
of the gold-edged lake.

Confession

"Know what I mean?"
said the clerk six times.
Six times I lied:
"Yes."

Her problem was this:
being new at her work,
she was unsure and unclear about my difficulty.
I felt embarrassed for her,
and, having no idea of her meaning,
I chose to lie.
So, six times I lied:
"Yes."

Now, I think the lies were venial.[3]
Since they came from kindness,
maybe they were even less than venial—
venial-minus, or so, just slipping in under the wire—
if you know what I mean.

---

3. Roman Catholic theology distinguishes a *venial sin* from a *mortal sin*, venial being slight, and mortal being potential deadly.

Lineage of Learning

God taught
both spider
and ant—most wondrous creatures.

Now He
uses ant
and spider as our teachers.

And if
you find in
this design a bit of sting,

recall:
you can't teach
ant or spider anything.

Or take
the thought from
just the other point of view:

no ant
or spider
ever learns a thing from you.

Prayer for Today

Come, great Shaper,
to my waiting mind,
come to fitly shape
some fragment
of Your wisdom,
carve in words
some contour of your
truth and beauty.

Design

Gossamer: a spider's web and its fabric,
a work of geometric beauty and detail,
a marvel of aesthetic engineering,
by weight a construction five times the strength of steel.

Unless your perspective is right,
or unless the sun illuminates the spider's web,
it is scarcely visible.
Though made to capture erring insects,
it will also cling to you,
encompassing your face or arm,
or holding to your clothes.

I have just read today's installment
of disheartening news.

News: a tangled, murky forest, where fear lurks
behind every creaking tree and whispering bush.

To snare me, Fear leaps from my computer,
sits on my work table, grins,
and dares me to be confident and happy.

And that requires me to contemplate
the ancient, all-enveloping web,
that strong, symmetrical gossamer,
created with imperishable strands of love and truth,
perfect in purpose and dumbfounding in design:
the eternal, encompassing web of supreme justice—
and, therefore, sweet repose.

November

Redbuds, bold in spring,
tremble under tumbling skies
in yellow pallor.

Wings

I walk today, companion to the slanting sun,
to honey locusts, grey and naked,
and to tapered pear trees, green and glossy, still.
Counterpart I am to maples, some opulent in orange,
some in flames, and some half clothed and ragged after frost.
I walk, obeying autumn's potent call,
the poignant lure of dying summer.

The Preacher was right:
a time there is to flourish and a time to die.
I muse: unrelenting Time itself
one day will end its long, constricting course—
will tick its last and fall asleep,
obedient to eternity's alarm.

I move on, sometimes shuffling leaves—
brown, enormous sycamore,
ubiquitous yellow maple, scarlet sassafras.
Now the road stops, and I stop, as well,
pondering the needless sign: ROAD ENDS.

Of course, every road ends
when the gravel or the pavement stops—
just as all trees go dormant when their sap grows cold,
or each season dies with the tipping of the earth.
Yes, a time there is for all things—even for dead ends,
though we mostly avoid them.
They accommodate better to wings than to walking.

I turn, dismissing the silly, redundant sign.
Again I contemplate the Preacher's list of mortal constrictions.
Yes, my leaves grow dry and wrinkled now,
my ration of sweet and shimmering autumns has run low,
and the long pavement of my days approaches
its unmarked and inevitable dead end.
But I am content: the wings, I know, are ready,
and my flight arrangements perfectly in place.

Squabble

Back and forth,
back and forth—
the hulking bruin in the zoo
pads back and forth incessantly.

Front feet here,
back feet there—
precise as soldiers in review,
each pad descends unerringly.

Each step exact,
no step untrue,
without concern for steps or you,
the bruin pads persistently.

Now, could it be
this padding bear
by some queer chance resembles you—
or, in clear fact, resembles me?

Doxology

In myriad-voiced dissonance
starlings, numberless, send from leafless trees
a fountain of raucous tweets and shrieks,
a wild cloud of raw cacophony,
an upward avalanche of chaotic sound:
one great wave of avian praise.

Then, suddenly, naked silence.

The starlings rise as one—
one swarming mass of black
that bursts from branches
and fountains into winter sunshine—
one gigantic, pliant cloud of shimmering black,
writhing like an enormous aerial amoeba.
The organism weaves and shrinks and grows
as multitudes of birds flash silver in the southern sun,
flying with marvelous precision and purpose,
writing with wings across the winter sky
their mystery of praise both agile and profound.

Lonesome

As Sages stooped in ecstasy and prayer,
perhaps, then, did the Holy Child compare
the far surpassing homage of His angel host?

When Joseph's Mary, blind to God's command,
His temple mission failed to understand,
did He then feel the pang of youthful solitude?

No friend He saw for forty desert days.
His only guest: the foe of all His ways;
bare solitude His sole companion as He fought.

Beloved were His twelve, who slowly learned.
"Do you not understand?" He urged—and yearned,
it seems, for oneness of their minds and hearts with Him.

Abandoned, lonesome in Gethsemane,
forsaken, heart-torn in extremity,
no friend, no Father, came to comfort or to aid.

Once-lonesome Lord, keen vigilance now keep,
lest, could it be, Your patient heart should weep
in lonesomeness for this, your weak and heart-slow sheep.

Riddle Pie

A gift it is, for you, your friends,
for anyone who happens by,
and plenty for your family.
Oh, my! Oh, my! It's huge, this pie.

Each gets one slice; it's large or small,
and, as would happen in a dream,
in some the filling tastes less rich,
and some seem topped with sweet whipped cream.

Two oddities imbue your slice:
you cannot calculate its size,
and though you surely savor it,
it never comes before your eyes.

Now, lest you view it as unfair
that slices vary in degree
of sweetness, size, or tempting taste,
remember that the pie is free.

You cannot give your piece away—
and if you tried, it would not do,
for once your single slice is gone,
well, so are you.

Evening Advice

Embrace what has been kind,
dismiss hurt or caprice,
set love first in your mind,
and then let sleep bring peace.

> *I will both lay me down in peace, and sleep:*
> *for thou, LORD, only makest me dwell in safety.*
> *—Psalm 4:8*

Self-Portrait

Maybe it is more than narcissism
that prompts artists to make self-portraits.

Bravely thinking that,
I decided to make one—a verbal mosaic.
But, much as I labored,
none of the word-stones wanted to fit,
and my mirror was smeared and sadly distorted.

So, the project died:
too little to see and too much smudge.
Besides that, I saw little opportunity for enhancement—
after all, flattery needs at least something to work with.

Well, I guess a psychiatrist would call that
a self-portrait.

Ecclesiastical Polity

The sober sexton minds
his keys and pews;
the prudent rector minds
his p's and q's.

Each week they meet for tea,
review the news,
and carefully appraise
dissenting views.

The service starts at nine;
the sexton smiles
while lacquered peace and love
pervade the aisles.

Some think the sermon long—
they yawn and writhe;
some find the pew too cold—
they keep their tithe.

The duo meets for tea.
They check the news
and narrowly assess
diverging views.

"This time," the sexton says,
"—and such a pity—
they'll give my keys and pews
to some committee."

"Ah, yes! Committees come—
and then they go.
And thus," the rector laughs,
"the blessings flow."

Spizzerinctum

"What we need around here is a little spizzerinctum,"
said the Baptist pastor to me one day as I sat at the organ.
I wondered, "Is that something plumbers use, or is it a brand of glue?
Maybe someone is sick and that's an anointing oil unique to Baptists."
(Baptists might suffer diseases unknown to other Protestants.)

He must have sensed my lack of comprehension:
"You know, some spizz, some real spizz!"

Well, I just kept practicing, didn't ask about the word,
and week by week for several years I kept playing for services,
enjoying his frank and vigorous style.

Years trooped by, and I never again saw Pastor Don.
Looking back, I realize that he was wishing
for something he already had:
spizzerinctum, his gift of infectious vigor,
a winsome part of his pastoral success.
But God had wrapped that gift inside another—innocence:
he was unaware that he exuded the very zeal he sought.

Now, maybe there is a lesson in that—
and maybe Socrates could make the point for us.
He wasn't exactly a Baptist,
but he was a sort of King James chap,
with language like, "Know thyself"
(which gives the thing a biblical ring).

But maybe sometimes it's better if you don't.

Timepiece

Like this old clock, loud-ticking, running slow,
my workings need a hand of restoration,
a hand that brings me steadiness and strength.

I have, through weeks and seasons year by year,
eagerly awaited Your approach,
welcoming the strength Your winding gives;
for all my fragile, subtly-working parts
have peace when once again You come to me
and firmly, gently turn my heartspring tight.

Again I wait for Your most needful hand.
Without Your care my inner workings stop,
and I lodge mute and useless in my place.

When You have made my halting heartspring strong,
when You have set my hands to working right,
then I will measure out my time with joy,
and You will look on me with fond delight.

Faith

"Daddy! help me! Daddy! help me!"
Her anguished voice echoes down fifty years.
Its desperation pursues me, still,
as I recall the nurse escorting me from the large hospital ward,
where they are tying her down
before stitching her forehead.

Everywhere such pleas of anguish
pursue helpless mothers
and haunt helpless fathers
as their children suffer sickness or separation,
as they endure perversion or persecution.

Helpless agony and helpless love:
ugly twins they are that mar this weeping world.

"Oh God! God, help me!"
cry His children torn by trial and pain.
But no one escorts Jesus from this wide ward.
With a mother's heart,
with a father's arms
He carries us and cures us,
He holds us and He helps us
in His mysterious way—
and in God's even more mysterious time.

> *He shall gather the lambs with his arm,*
> *and carry them in his bosom.*
> *—Isaiah 40:11*

Resurrection

Some few pale leaves, dry, shriveling,
to barren branches thin and hopeless cling,
cling through frost-filled morns, sunless noons,
and dreamless nights beneath small, sterile moons.

But yet each quaking twig bears bold
and eager buds to mock impending cold;
for as they face cruel winter's sting,
they share the heartwood's certainty of spring.

www.ingramcontent.com/pod-product-compliance
Lightning Source LLC
Chambersburg PA
CBHW061511040426
42450CB00008B/1557